To _____

From _____

Other giftbooks by Helen Exley:
Passion   I Love You
The Kiss   Love Quotations
True Love...

Published simultaneously in 1996 by Exley Publications in Great Britain, and
Exley Giftbooks in the USA.
Copyright © Helen Exley 1996
The moral right of the author has been asserted

12   11   10   9   8   7

Border illustrations by Juliette Clarke
Edited and pictures selected by Helen Exley

ISBN 1-85015-798-7

Picture research by Image Select International.
Typeset by Delta, Watford.
Printed in China.

Exley Publications Ltd, 16 Chalk Hill, Watford, Herts WD1 4BN, UK.
Exley Publications LLC, 232 Madison Avenue, Suite 1206, NY 10016, USA.

THE
*W*ICKED
LITTLE BOOK OF
QUOTES

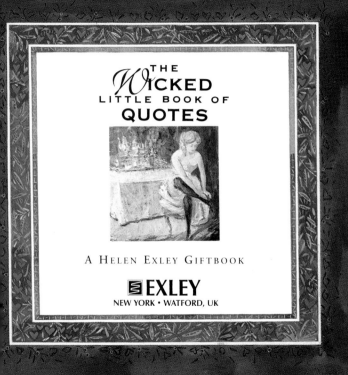

A HELEN EXLEY GIFTBOOK

▤EXLEY
NEW YORK • WATFORD, UK

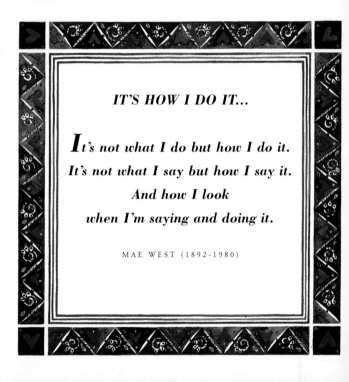

IT'S HOW I DO IT...

It's not what I do but how I do it.
It's not what I say but how I say it.
And how I look
when I'm saying and doing it.

MAE WEST (1892-1980)

I kissed my first girl and smoked my first cigarette on the same day. I haven't had time for tobacco since.

ARTURO TOSCANINI (1867-1957)

Sex got me into trouble from the age of 15: I'm hoping that by the time I'm 70 I'll straighten it out.

HAROLD ROBBINS, b.1916

If I had to live my life again, I'd make the same mistakes, only sooner.

TALLULAH BANKHEAD (1903-1968)

ONE-TRACK MINDS

Men are those creatures with two legs and eight hands.

JAYNE MANSFIELD

Give a man a free hand and he'll run it all over you.

MAE WEST (1892-1980)

A student undergoing a word-association test was asked why a snowstorm put him in mind of sex. He replied frankly: "Because everything does."

HONOR TRACY

I will find you twenty lascivious turtles ere

one chaste man.

WILLIAM SHAKESPEARE (1564-1616),
FROM *"THE MERRY WIVES OF WINDSOR"*

The average male thinks about sex every 11

minutes while he's awake.

DR. PATRICK GREENE

When I glimpse the backs of women's knees

I seem to hear the first movement of

Beethoven's *Pastoral Symphony*.

FROM THE *"DAILY MAIL"*

I have bursts of being a lady, but it
doesn't last long.

SHELLEY WINTERS

Letter to George Burns: "Dear George,
I've been married for eight years.
I love my wife very much, but she's a
nymphomaniac. What should I do?"
George Burns: "Stop writing letters and
count your blessings."

[In a letter to Thomas Carlyle, her husband:]
I am not at all the sort of person you and I
took me for.

JANE CARLYLE (1801-1866)

My mother said it was simple to keep a man,
you must be a maid in the living room, a
cook in the kitchen and a whore in the
bedroom. I said I'd hire the other two and
take care of the bedroom bit.

JERRY HALL

To err is human, but it feels divine.

MAE WEST (1892-1980)

Men aren't attracted to me by my mind,
they're attracted by what I *don't* mind.

GYPSY ROSE LEE

Between two evils, I always
pick the one I never
tried before.

MAE WEST (1892-1980),
FROM *"KLONDIKE ANNIE"*

My mother used to say, Delia, if S-E-X ever rears its ugly head, close your eyes before you see the rest of it.

ALAN AYCKBOURN, b.1939,
FROM *"BEDROOM FARCE"*

Pray, what was Nature thinking of when she made this? She almost puts herself on a level with those who draw in privies.

HENRY DAVID THOREAU (1817-1862),
FROM *"JOURNALS"*

One of them would call it her little dille, her staff of love, her quillety, her faucetin, her dandilollie: Another her peen, her jolly kyle, her bableret, her membretoon, her quickset imp: Another again, her branch of coral, her female adamant, her placket-racket, her Cyprian sceptre, her jewel for ladies: and some of the women would give it these names, my bunguetee, my stopple too, my

busherusher, my gallant wimble, my pretty boarer, my coney-burrow ferret, my little

piercer, my augretine, my dangling hangers, down right
to it, stiff and stout, in and to, my pusher, dresser,
pouting stick, my honey pipe, my pretty pillicock, linkie
pinkie, futilletie, my lusty andouille and crimson
chitterlin, my little couille bredouille, my pretty rogue.

FRANCOIS RABELAIS (C.1494-C.1530),
FROM *"GARGANTUA AND PANTAGRUEL"*

Lead me not into temptation;
I can find the way myself.

RITA MAE BROWN

I lost my reputation young,
but never missed it.

MAE WEST
(1892-1980)

I generally avoid temptation, unless I can't resist it.

MAE WEST (1892-1980)

The phone went in the house and I answered it and this voice said, "Hello, how would you like a dirty weekend in Paris?" And then there was a silence and the voice said, "I'm sorry. Have I shocked you?" And I said, "God no –
I was just packing."

HELEN LEDERER

BLISSFUL IGNORANCE

Lost in last July, behind the late Sir George Whitmore's, a maidenhead, the owner never having missed it till the person who since married her expected to have had it as part of her dowry. If the pastry cook in Fleet Street, who is supposed to have brought it away out of a frolic, will restore it again to Mrs. Sarah Stroakings, at the Cow-House at Islington, he shall be treated with a syllabub.

FROM *"THE FEMALE TATLER"*

Dear Marje, If a girl has intercourse and then has nothing more to do with boys for a year, can she become a virgin again?

LETTER FROM "HOPEFUL", IN THE *DAILY MIRROR*

Finally, while on the subject of blissful ignorance, we should mention the case of the Taiwan mother of six who was found sobbing hysterically in a Formosa street in March 1983. Asked what was her predicament, she replied, "I won't have any more children. A neighbour has just told me what causes them."

GRAHAM AND LYNNE JONES, FROM *"I LOVE SEX I HATE SEX"*

T**here are two good reasons why men go to see her.
Those are enough.**

HOWARD HUGHES (1905-1976),
ON JANE RUSSELL

Dramatic art in her opinion is knowing how to fill a sweater.

BETTE DAVIS (1908-1989),
ON JAYNE MANSFIELD

If I hadn't had them, I would have had some made.

DOLLY PARTON, b.1946, ON HER BREASTS

... her figure described a set of parabolas that could cause cardiac arrest in a yak.

WOODY ALLEN, b.1935, FROM *"GETTING EVEN"*

My boyfriend says my dress is so tight he can hardly breathe.

ANON

In my sex fantasy, nobody ever loves me for my mind.

NORA EPHRON, b.1941

If I told you you have a beautiful body, you wouldn't hold it against me would you?

DAVID FISHER

What comes first in a relationship is lust –
then more lust.

JACQUELINE BISSET

He kissed the plump mellow yellor smellor
melons of her rump, on each plump
melonous hemisphere, in their mellow
yellow furrow, with obscure prolonged
provocative melonsmellonous osculation.

JAMES JOYCE (1882-1941)

It is monstrously indecent. One wonders
how two self-respecting people could face
each other after performing it.

W. T. STEAD (1849-1912)

These two did oftentimes do the two-backed beast together, joyfully rubbing and frotting their bacon against one another....

FRANÇOIS RABELAIS (c.1494-c.1530), FROM *"GARGANTUA AND PANTAGRUEL"*

Isn't it interesting how the sounds are the same for an awful nightmare and great sex?

RUE McCLANAHAN, AS BLANCHE DEVEREAUX, FROM *"THE GOLDEN GIRLS"*

I've tried several varieties of sex. The conventional position makes me claustrophobic. And the others either give me a stiff neck or lockjaw.

TALLULAH BANKHEAD (1903-1968)

Is there any greater or keener pleasure than physical love? No, nor any which is more unreasonable.

PLATO (427-327 B.C.)

HEALTH HAZARD!

… keeping a clean bill of health remains the prime non-spiritual justification for celibacy. Is it not true that this base animal instinct can give you acne, blindness, whooping cough, gout, housemaid's knee, tennis elbow, Achilles heel, and a succession of allergies reading like the menu in a French Grand Hotel?"

GRAHAM AND LYNNE JONES,
FROM *"I LOVE SEX I HATE SEX"*

He who immerses himself in sexual intercourse will be assailed by premature ageing, his strength will wane, his eyes will weaken, and a bad odour will emit from his mouth and his armpits, his teeth will fall out and many other maladies will afflict him.

MAIMONIDES, FROM *"MISHNEH TORAH"*

If brevity is the soul of wit, your penis must be a riot.

DONNA GEPHART

Porfirio Rubirosa was a literally priapic rogue and liar whose member was said to be so large that waiters in Paris referred to large pepper mills as Rubirosas.

FROM THE *"NEW YORK OBSERVER"*

Is that a pistol in your pocket, or are you just glad to see me?

MAE WEST (1892-1980)

NO SEX PLEASE!

The perfect hostess will see to it that the works of male and female authors be properly separated on her bookshelves. Their proximity, unless they happen to be married, should not be tolerated.

LADY GOUGH, ETIQUETTE OF 1836

Any woman who shall impose upon, seduce and betray into matrimony any of His Majesty's subjects by virtue of scents, paints, cosmetic washes, artificial teeth, false hair, iron stays, hoops, high-heeled shoes, or bolstered hips, shall incur the penalty against witchcraft, and the marriage... shall be null and void.

ENGLISH ACT OF PARLIAMENT

At no time did history say "no" to sex, of course, quite like the Victorian era, when sofas were banned as "sex chairs", midwives delivered babies under shrouds, women bathed from protective "machines" in twenty-yard cotton cocoons, books by male and female authors were separated on the bookshelves, and no polite person would dream of offering a lady a chicken "leg" (the very word a crime). One Methodist minister in St. Martin's Lane, London, even tied the legs of his cockerel together so the henhouse was free of sin on the Sabbath.

GRAHAM AND LYNNE JONES,
FROM "*I LOVE SEX I HATE SEX*"

But all my life I have been attracted to nice girls, the kind you aren't supposed to *do it* to, and they, too, have been brought up, at least in my generation, thinking that they shouldn't *do it* either. How *it* ever gets done between nice people is a mystery to me.

ALLAN SHERMAN

I CAN STRUT MY PUDDING

SPREAD MY GREASE WITH EASE

'CAUSE I KNOW MY ONIONS

THAT'S WHY I ALWAYS PLEASE

NELLIE FLORENCE, FROM
"JACKSONVILLE BLUES"

YOU CAN SHAKE

JUST LIKE IT WOULD A TREE

THE WAY YOU SHAKE IT

IT'S PLEASING ME

JUST LET ME TELL YOU

A THING OR TWO

A PLENTY OF PEOPLE SHAKE IT

BUT NOT LIKE YOU

ANNA BELL,
"SHAKE IT, BLACK BOTTOM"

SHE'S NO LADY!

WHAT'S A NICE PLACE LIKE THIS DOING IN A GIRL LIKE YOU?

AMERICAN CATCH-PHRASE

IT TAKES A LOT OF EXPERIENCE FOR A GIRL TO KISS LIKE A BEGINNER.

ANONYMOUS

A LADY IS ONE WHO NEVER SHOWS HER UNDERWEAR UNINTENTIONALLY.

LILLIAN DAY,
FROM *"KISS AND TELL"*

MY COMPUTER-DATING BUREAU CAME
UP WITH A PERFECT GENTLEMAN.
STILL, I'VE GOT ANOTHER THREE GOES.

SALLY POPLIN

ONE MORE DRINK AND I'LL BE
UNDER THE HOST.

DOROTHY PARKER
(1893-1967)

A RIDDLE

A strange thing hangs by a man's thigh under its
master's clothes. It is pierced in front, is stiff and
hard, has a good fixed place. When the man lifts his
own garment up above his knee, he wishes to visit
with the head of this hanging instrument the
familiar hole which it, when of equal length, has
often filled before.

FROM *"THE EXETER BOOK OF RIDDLES"*, c.975

(probable answer: key)

UP WITH PETTICOATS,
DOWN WITH DRAWERS!
YOU TICKLE MINE
AND I'LL TICKLE YOURS!

AND HERE AND THERE I HAD HER,
AND EVERYWHERE I HAD HER,
HER TOY WAS SUCH, THAT EVERY TOUCH
WOULD MAKE A LOVER MADDER.

SIR GEORGE ETHEREGE (1635-1692),
FROM *"SHE WOULD IF SHE COULD"*

HOORAY! HOORAY! THE FIRST OF MAY!
OUTDOOR SCREWING BEGINS TODAY!

FOLK RHYME

I am in favor of preserving the French habit of kissing ladies' hands – after all, one must start somewhere.

SACHA GUITRY (1885-1957)

The kiss is a wordless articulation of desire whose object lies in the future, and somewhat to the south.

LANCE MORROW

A man may talk inspiringly to a woman about love in the abstract – but the look in his eyes is always perfectly concrete.

HELEN ROWLAND (1876-1950),
FROM *"PERSONALLY SPEAKING"*

Boy meets girl; girl gets boy into pickle;
boy gets pickle into girl.

JACK WOODFORD, ON FICTION PLOTS

In order to avoid being called a flirt,
she always yielded easily.

CHARLES-MAURICE DE
TALLEYRAND-PERIGORD (1754-1838)

She's the kind of girl who climbed the
ladder of success wrong by wrong.

MAE WEST (1892-1980)

Good girls go to heaven.
Bad girls go everywhere.

HELEN GURLEY BROWN

THEY THINK IT'S ALL OVER...

WHAT A JOLLY BUNCH THEY WERE, AND THE ONLY ONE WHO WASN'T SMILING WAS SOLLY, A 70-YEAR-OLD TAXI DRIVER, WHO WAS STARING MOURNFULLY AT HIS PRICK AND INTONING: "WE WERE BORN TOGETHER. WE GREW UP TOGETHER. WE GOT MARRIED TOGETHER. WHY, OH WHY, DID YOU HAVE TO DIE BEFORE ME?"

JEFFREY BERNARD, FROM *"LOW LIFE"*

I HAVE EVERYTHING I HAD TWENTY
YEARS AGO – EXCEPT NOW IT'S ALL
LOWER.

GYPSY ROSE LEE

AS A YOUNG MAN I USED TO HAVE FOUR
SUPPLE MEMBERS AND ONE STIFF ONE.
NOW I HAVE FOUR STIFF AND ONE
SUPPLE.

HENRI, DUC D'AUMALE

A girl can wait for the right man
to come along but in the meantime
that still doesn't mean she can't
have a wonderful time with all
the wrong ones.

CHER

Love is the answer; but while you are
waiting for the answer, sex raises some
pretty good questions.

WOODY ALLEN, b.1935

The only chaste woman is one who has not been asked.

SPANISH PROVERB

Diane: "My heart's saying 'yes', my mind's saying 'no'."
Sam: "Why don't you let some other part of your body break the tie?"

FROM *"CHEERS"*

She who hesitates… is won.

A. DILLON-MALONE

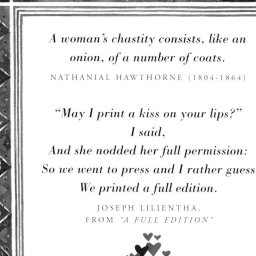

A woman's chastity consists, like an onion, of a number of coats.

NATHANIAL HAWTHORNE (1804-1864)

"May I print a kiss on your lips?"
I said,
And she nodded her full permission:
So we went to press and I rather guess
We printed a full edition.

JOSEPH LILIENTHA,
FROM *"A FULL EDITION"*

The follies which a man regrets most in his
life are those which he didn't commit when
he had the opportunity.

HELEN ROWLAND (1876-1950),
FROM *"REFELCTIONS OF A BACHELOR GIRL"*

If you obey all the rules, you miss all the fun.

KATHARINE HEPBURN, b.1909

A LITTLE SHE STROVE...

A little she strove,

and much repented

And whispering "I'll ne'er consent"

– consented.

LORD BYRON (1788-1824)

Acknowledgements: The publishers are grateful for permission to reproduce copyright material. Whilst every effort has been made to trace copyright holders, the publishers would be pleased to hear from any not here acknowledged. GRAHAM and LYNNE JONES: Extracts from *I Love Sex I Hate Sex,* © Graham and Lynne Jones, reprinted by permission of Peters, Frazer & Dunlop.